What Were the Shark Attacks of 1916?

by Nico Medina

illustrated by Tim Foley

Penguin Workshop

For Audrey and Connor,
the sweetest beachcombers—NM

For Trout—TF

PENGUIN WORKSHOP
An imprint of Penguin Random House LLC, New York

First published in the United States of America by Penguin Workshop,
an imprint of Penguin Random House LLC, New York, 2024

Visit us online at penguinrandomhouse.com.

Library of Congress Control Number: 2023039987

Printed in the United States of America

ISBN 9780593521588 (paperback)   10 9 8 7 6 5 4 3 2 1 WOR
ISBN 9780593521595 (library binding)   10 9 8 7 6 5 4 3 2 1 WOR

Contents

What Were the Shark Attacks of 1916?

July 11, 1916—Matawan, New Jersey

Fourteen-year-old Rensselaer "Renny" Cartan Jr. was sweating. It was almost two o'clock—the hottest time of day, and Renny had been working at his dad's lumber and coal business since morning. Usually around now, the factory owners and shopkeepers of Matawan, New Jersey, allowed their young employees a quick break to cool off in the creek. Soon enough, Renny was released from his work duties.

He met his younger cousin Johnson, who stocked shelves at his dad's department store. The boys met some friends and headed down Main Street.

The factories along Matawan Creek manufactured a wide variety of goods, from candy and matches to pianos and pottery. The creek was also used to transport fresh produce to New York City, thirty miles away.

But for Renny and his buddies, Matawan Creek was a place to have fun.

The boys headed down the creek's muddy embankment. Their favorite spot was a small cove at a bend in the creek, a sort of private swimming hole. It was next to the old limeworks, a processing plant where mountains of oyster shells had once been crushed into powder. But industry and pollution had killed off the area's oysters, and the limeworks had closed.

Within seconds of arriving, the boys had tossed their clothes into the grass and leaped naked into the water. Recent heavy rains had kicked up sediment from the creek bed, making the water murkier than usual. But who cared how muddy the water was, as long as it was cool?

Renny climbed onto a dock piling. As he joked with his friends, he began to lose his balance.

He had no idea as he fell what awaited him beneath the surface.

The water was neck-deep. Suddenly, Renny was clipped by a huge, hard object whooshing in front of him. Sharp pricks of pain bloomed across his chest. The water around him turned red.

Panic washed over Renny. Wide-eyed, he spotted the largest fish he'd ever seen.

It was a *shark*! Swimming in the creek among his friends!

Renny screamed and rushed out of the water. His chest was bleeding from wounds caused by the shark's abrasive skin.

Sharks' bodies are covered by V-shaped, toothlike scales called denticles that help them swim quickly and quietly. Sharkskin is so rough, it was once used as sandpaper.

On shore, Renny's friends tried to calm him. No one *else* had seen the shark. Maybe a branch had scraped Renny.

But Renny *knew* he'd been struck by a shark,

just like those two men at the Jersey Shore.

Five days earlier, in the seaside resort town of Spring Lake, a man was swimming in the Atlantic Ocean when he was brutally attacked and killed by a shark. Five days before that, *another* man had been killed in Beach Haven. Nothing like this had ever happened before in the United States, and it was all over the nation's newspapers.

But Matawan was a mile upriver from the closest body of salt water. How could a shark have traveled this far inland?

Renny's cousin and friends returned to the water, as Renny pleaded with them not to. They wouldn't listen. No *way* had Renny seen a shark! His imagination must've gotten the better of him.

Renny walked home to get his cuts bandaged. He feared for his friends. But they were lucky that day.

When a shark made its way up the creek the following day, the people of Matawan wouldn't be so lucky.

CHAPTER 1
Apex Predator

Some believe the shark that slashed Renny Cartan—and the shark or sharks that killed the men on the Jersey Shore—was a young great white shark.

Great white shark

Also known simply as *white sharks*, these fearsome predators get their name from their white bellies, which help camouflage (or hide) them when viewed from below. The white color helps the shark blend in with the sunlight. The top of a white shark is dark, making it harder to spot from above.

The white shark's scientific name, *Carcharodon carcharias*, means "biter with the jagged teeth"—and the name fits. Its razor-sharp teeth are serrated, like steak knives. These two-inch-long triangular chompers are designed to slice through flesh and bone. And with jaws so strong, they can exert four thousand pounds of pressure per square inch—six times more powerful than a lion's jaws. A single white shark bite is often deadly.

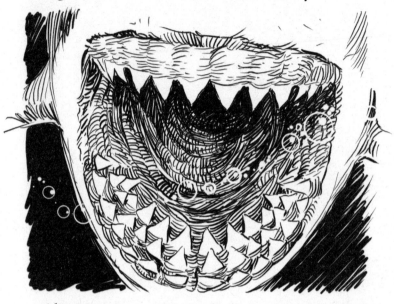

About twenty-six teeth line a white shark's top jaw, with around twenty-four along the bottom. Behind the front set of teeth lie up to six additional rows of softer "baby teeth"—that's as many as 350 teeth! Every ten to fourteen days, each set of front teeth falls out and is replaced by the next row.

Great whites are truly great in size. Males grow up to fourteen feet long. Females can be more than twenty feet and weigh five thousand pounds! They are even *born* big—up to five feet long and eighty-five pounds.

Male, 11–13 feet

Female, 15–16 feet

Human, 6 feet

Average lengths of great white sharks

White sharks don't lay eggs; they give live birth. Females carry two to twelve pups in their womb for up to fourteen months. Sometimes pups will eat one or more of their siblings before they are born. The surviving pups must swim away quickly, so they don't become a snack for their mother!

A white shark never stops swimming. Unlike other fish, it has no swim bladder (an internal expandable sac) to help keep it afloat. If it stops swimming, it sinks.

Young white sharks feed mainly on fish, rays, and other sharks. As they grow, they begin to eat sea mammals, like seals, sea lions, and dead whale carcasses. These animals are rich in blubber, which the sharks store as energy in their livers. After a big, fatty meal, white sharks can go a month or two before feeding again.

When it's hunting, a white shark goes on high alert. It can smell a meal one-third of a mile away.

It can also detect electromagnetic pulses in the water. This sixth sense is called electroreception. A special organ under the nose receives signals from these vibrations from miles away and guides the shark toward its prey.

Great whites are ambush hunters that surprise their victims from below. When a shark spots a potential meal, it waits for just the right moment. Then, in a burst of speed up to forty miles per hour, its torpedo-like body rockets toward the surface.

The shark rolls its pitch-black eyeballs back into its head to protect them from thrashing flippers. After catching its prey in its jaws, the shark will sometimes breach—break the surface—flying up to ten feet in the air.

After that first ferocious bite, white sharks often swim away and wait for the animal to bleed to death. This saves the shark's energy and prevents injury by its struggling prey. White sharks are careful, practiced hunters, not mindless killing machines, as often portrayed in the movies.

They are also world travelers. White sharks have been known to swim from the Gulf of Mexico to Massachusetts. Some migrate between California and Hawaii, more than two thousand miles! They usually spend colder months in temperate or tropical areas. (Some scientists believe white sharks are born and grow up in these waters.) When the weather warms, they move to cooler zones.

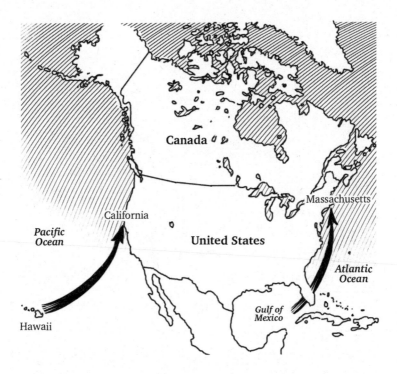

Why travel such distances? For food, of course! And where there are seals, there are sharks. Cape Cod, Massachusetts, is home to a large and growing seal population during the summer months. The Farallon Islands, thirty miles off San Francisco, California, host thousands of seals and sea lions, attracting hungry white sharks every autumn.

Seals on Cape Cod, Massachusetts

White sharks have been stalking the oceans for up to ten million years. (Humans have existed for only about three hundred thousand.) In that time, they have evolved to become apex predators.

Apex means "the top." An apex predator has few natural enemies.

Sharks have been worshipped as gods—and feared as demons—since ancient times. Native Hawaiians offered human sacrifices to appease the shark gods. Workers building the US naval base at Pearl Harbor discovered the remains of a four-acre underwater pen, enclosed by lava rocks. This marine arena is believed to have hosted death matches between men, armed only with short spears, and sharks. (The sharks usually won.)

Shark attacks on humans today are extremely rare. Worldwide, between fifty and one hundred occur annually; five to ten are deadly. A person is thirty times more likely to die from a lightning strike—and *one thousand* times more likely to drown.

Still, attacks happen—and they follow patterns. Attacks come from below or behind. Surfers in dark wet suits are sometimes targeted, because they resemble seals. A person swimming solo— like a lone sea lion, separated from its pack—is also more likely to attract a shark's attention. More than eight out of every ten attacks occur when there are no other swimmers within ten feet.

Megalodon

Sharks have been around since before the dinosaurs, and the great white has not always been the ocean's apex predator. It once shared the seas with a much larger shark known as *Otodus megalodon.*

Megalodon evolved about twenty million years ago. Its name means "big tooth"—its teeth were

Megalodon, 58.7 feet

more than six inches long! Megalodon was the largest predatory fish to ever exist. It was sixty feet long—three times longer than a white shark!—and it weighed more than sixty tons. It fed on dolphins, whales, and other sharks—maybe even great whites! Recently, megalodon has been the subject of big-budget action movies, but that's just science fiction. This ocean monster has been extinct for 3.6 million years.

Great white shark, 16 feet

Megalodon and
great white shark sizes

Often, the shark strikes fast and swims away after one bite. But that is not what happened in New Jersey in 1916.

CHAPTER 2
Summer at the Shore

Nineteen sixteen was an exciting time in the United States. The steam-powered engine, railroads, and assembly lines had transformed the young nation—two generations out of the Civil War—into a global economic powerhouse.

New inventions were changing people's daily lives. Electric toasters, vacuum cleaners, and refrigerators. Alarm clocks, telephones, elevators, and even movies!

Telephone, 1916

Millions of immigrants flocked to rapidly growing cities. They crowded into cramped and often dirty tenement apartments and got jobs in the factories that seemed to be popping up everywhere.

On bustling city streets, people competed for space with horse-drawn carriages, streetcars, and the latest mode of transportation: automobiles!

Since 1900, the number of cars in the nation had increased from eight thousand to more than three *million*.

These changes brought some problems, though. Cities were crowded, and diseases spread quickly. That summer, there was an outbreak of polio in New York City.

At the time, polio was commonly known as infantile paralysis because it mostly affected children under the age of five. It began with a sore throat, aches, and fever. Most children would recover, but for others, the limbs (arms and legs) would become paralyzed, meaning they could no longer move. Sometimes, the larynx (part of the throat) would seize up, choking the child to death.

Today, we know polio can be spread by infected people or by food or water contaminated with sewage. But in 1916, there was confusion and panic—and no cure. (A vaccine was not developed until the 1950s.) Schools, ballparks, and theaters closed. People in surrounding areas feared the disease might come to their town next.

Doctors believed the best way to cure the disease—and prevent its spread in the first place—was to flee the filthy, overcrowded cities

and breathe fresh, clean air. With the summer shaping up to be a scorcher, there was one place everybody could go: the beach! And with newly built train lines crisscrossing the nation, getting to the ocean—even just for the day—was within more people's reach than ever.

Resort towns had been popping up along the Jersey Shore since the late 1800s. By 1916, some had become large, extravagant cities. Atlantic City was home to four hundred hotels that could host fifty thousand guests. One hotel restaurant's ceiling was also the glass bottom of a sunlit aquarium! The city of Asbury Park was lined by grand boulevards that may have reminded visitors of the streets of Paris.

Traymore Hotel, Atlantic City

The Jersey Shore was America's summertime playground, earning visits from several presidents. Atlantic City built the world's first boardwalk, a beachside "Main Street" everyone could enjoy. All sorts of entertainment and distractions could be found there. Sandcastle building competitions, a new fad, were all the rage. Jazz, a new kind of music from New Orleans, could be heard in bars and nightclubs.

There was even saltwater taffy, which had first been made there in the 1880s!

One playwright said Atlantic City was "all the seaside pleasure cities of the world rolled into one, then raised to the third power."

Ocean swimming was a rather new pastime. It had only become popular in the last twenty or so years. Still, many upper-class Americans considered it lowly and dangerous. Until the turn of the century, there were even separate swimming hours for men and women! But times were changing.

Beachgoers flocked to the ocean that summer looking for fun and fresh air. But many didn't consider the risks. Most Americans couldn't swim, and drownings were frequent. The shallowest areas near the shore were roped off to give bathers something to hold for safety.

Hardly anyone worried about sharks. Aside from a photograph in a book or magazine, most people had never seen a real-life shark. And *no one* had ever heard of an attack occurring this far north. Maybe in warmer, tropical waters . . . but in New Jersey?

An ocean away in Europe, World War I was raging. If Americans were worried about anything lurking in the water, it was German U-boats—submarines that had been monitoring Canadian and US supply ships up and down the Eastern Seaboard. "He kept us out of war" was

President Woodrow Wilson

President Woodrow Wilson's reelection campaign slogan that year. But people wondered how long the United States could remain neutral and not participate in the war.

Sharks were the last thing on anyone's minds that summer. Until the unthinkable happened.

Beach Fashion

Beachwear in the early 1900s was very different from today's fashions. Men wore black tank tops and long swim tights that reached just above the knee. Women's bathing costumes were dresses with collars, often made of wool or flannel, covering most of the body. In 1916, the more form-fitting "swimsuit" was introduced. This new look was more revealing and exposed the woman's arms and legs.

Some towns began to make rules about "acceptable" beachwear. In Atlantic City, swimsuits weren't allowed on the boardwalk or in hotels. Men could be arrested for the crime of going shirtless. Bathhouses were built near the beach, where people could rinse off and change.

"Decency police" patrolled the beaches, measuring the distance of the hem of a woman's bathing costume above her knee, to make sure it wasn't too scandalously revealing. Still, some people found small ways to rebel. When the cops weren't looking, they rolled their bathing socks down below their knees!

Women bathers in the early 1900s

CHAPTER 3
The First Attack

July 1, 1916—Beach Haven, New Jersey

Beach Haven was built on Long Beach Island, six miles from the mainland of New Jersey. Advertised as having the freshest air, the town

was newly connected to Philadelphia by four daily roundtrip express train rides—and it was expecting a busy summer. Two hundred shade trees were planted to welcome visitors, and the boardwalk was being widened.

At the Engleside Hotel, where the well-to-do Vansant family of Philadelphia would be staying, all 150 rooms were booked from the Fourth of July through Labor Day in September.

It was twenty-three-year-old Charles Vansant's last summer as a single man. That autumn, he'd be married. Soon, summers at the Shore with just his sisters and parents would be a thing of the past.

Charles Vansant

After the family checked in, Vansant changed and headed to the beach. It was already after five o'clock, but there was still time to swim before dinner. Vansant's family watched him from the boardwalk.

On the beach, Vansant met a red Chesapeake Bay retriever, and they played in the surf. More people joined the Vansants on the boardwalk. The assembled crowd cheered as the duo swam past the other bathers, then out past the big ocean waves known as breakers.

Beneath the surface, something else eyed Vansant and the retriever with great interest.

Vibrations from the dog's frenzied paddling and the man's strokes had sent electromagnetic pulses into the open ocean . . . and drawn a shark to shore to investigate.

In his full-body all-black bathing costume, Vansant might have looked like a seal to the hungry shark. Monitoring the two objects from below, the shark bided its time.

Today, we know that swimming with a dog increases the odds of an attack. But Charles

Vansant wouldn't have been aware of this.

The dog sensed something in the water with them—something *big*. It turned suddenly and began paddling to shore. Vansant called for the dog, but it kept swimming. Laughing, the man decided he'd had enough, too, and followed it.

As Vansant approached the shore, observers spotted a large, dark fin pierce the surface behind him.

Was it a porpoise?

No. It was something far more sinister.

"Watch out!" they cried. But it was too late.

The shark grabbed Vansant's left leg, just below the knee. At first, some people didn't believe his hair-raising screams were for real. Vansant was standing in just three and a half feet of water, and they thought he was playing a prank. But he was fighting for his life, and the shark wasn't letting go. It bit down harder, puncturing a main artery and ripping out Vansant's calf muscle.

Suddenly, the shark released the man. It lurked in the surf, waiting for him to bleed out.

Local lifeguard Alexander Ott raced into the water. Ott grabbed Vansant and began pulling him ashore. To his horror, he felt a tug in the opposite direction. The shark had returned to claim its meal!

Two more men joined arms with Ott, forming a human chain. A bloody tug-of-war ensued.

Witnesses say the shark was blue-gray or black and about nine feet long—and that it released Vansant only after being dragged nearly out of the water, its belly scraping against the sand.

Blood gushed from Vansant's half-eaten leg. Ott made a tourniquet (a bandage to stop the flow of blood) from the fabric of a woman's dress, but it barely slowed the bleeding.

Charles's father, Dr. Eugene Vansant, ran to his son. Other doctors staying at the hotel were summoned. The closest hospital was thirty miles away. They feared Vansant wouldn't survive the ride.

Charles Vansant was brought to the hotel manager's office. The door was taken off its hinges and laid across a desk. On this makeshift operating table, Dr. Vansant cleaned and bandaged his son's wounds. But there was no saving him.

At 6:45 p.m., just an hour after entering the ocean with his whole summer and his whole life ahead of him, Charles Vansant died.

CHAPTER 4
The $500 Bet

That night, the Engleside Hotel was abuzz. Usually, guests passed their time writing postcards, playing cards, reading, or painting. But on July 1, all anyone could do was talk about the gruesome attack on the young man from Philadelphia.

Some guests canceled their vacations, many deciding to visit the mountains instead. The hotel owner reassured everyone there was no cause for concern. The next day, workers would begin to install protective netting around the Engleside's beach.

Reporters questioned guests and witnesses. Some said it was a shark. Others weren't so sure. Local fishermen suggested it had been a large tuna, sailfish, or even a sea turtle.

The former director of Philadelphia's aquarium told a local paper that if it *had* been a shark, it was probably trying to attack the dog. Sharks rarely come to shore, he said, and bathers need not worry.

The *New York Times* reported on the incident three days later—at the bottom of the last page. The article described it as an "attack by fish."

Still, the cause of death on Charles Vansant's death certificate was clear: "bitten by a shark while bathing," the first time such a thing had been recorded in American history.

Beach Haven officials didn't alert neighboring towns about the attack. New Jersey beaches remained open, and life returned to normal. In Atlantic City, fifty thousand bathers frolicked in the surf the day after Vansant's death. Eleven of them had to be rescued—not from sharks, but from drowning.

Why wasn't there a more alarming and

widespread response to such an unusual and horrific event? Because to many people at that time, legends of man-eating sharks were just that: legends.

Stories of shark attacks in ancient times were plentiful. In Italy, around 700 BCE, a potter painted a vase depicting a man being eaten by a large fish. In 492 BCE, the Greek historian Herodotus wrote of "marine monsters" that attacked men at sea. In 1916, however, few believed sharks attacked humans. Scientists thought shark bites were poisonous and their jaws were too weak to crush human bone.

How wrong they were!

Historically, Americans had always been quite frightened by sharks. But a New York City millionaire named Hermann Oelrichs changed that.

Hermann Oelrichs

Lifeguards on the Shore

Due to its shifting sandbars and strong currents, the Jersey Shore has been the site of many shipwrecks. By 1815, small bands of volunteers—the earliest "lifeguards"—rescued people from ships that had run aground. In 1849, the US government built eight lifeboat stations along the shore, and by 1874, there were forty.

As sailing vessels were replaced with steamer ships and shipwrecks became less frequent, rescuers' focus shifted to swimmers at rapidly growing resort towns along the coast. Atlantic City hired its first beach-patrol lifeguards—called surfmen—in 1872. By 1884, most towns employed groups of surfmen, all trained in resuscitation and first aid. In 1915, they became part of the newly formed US Coast Guard. New Jersey lifeguards still perform thousands of rescues each year.

In the late 1800s, Oelrichs was one of the nation's most rich and powerful men. Six feet tall and two hundred pounds, with a thick handlebar mustache, he cut an impressive figure. An accomplished sportsman and amateur boxer, Oelrichs popularized the game of lacrosse, and introduced Americans to the game of polo. He even once wrestled a caged lion!

Every summer, to the delight of reporters and curious spectators, Oelrichs made a five-mile "shark-chasing" swim off the Jersey Shore. He claimed to be scaring off cowardly sharks. Oelrichs loved hosting lavish parties to boast about his adventures.

Oelrichs was so certain sharks posed no threat to humans that in 1891, he made a bet with the American public. He took out an ad in the *New York Sun*, offering $500—a sizable sum at the time!—to anyone who could prove that a shark had ever attacked a living person north of Cape

Hatteras, North Carolina.

That July, Oelrichs invited a group of wealthy friends—including future president Theodore Roosevelt—aboard his steam-powered yacht. As the party cruised out to sea, Oelrichs made a surprise announcement: They were looking for sharks!

The guests were shaken. They knew their host's reward in the *Sun* had not been claimed. And they'd heard of Oelrichs's encounters with sharks. But that was all in good fun. What would

happen one hundred miles out in the open ocean?

A school of sharks appeared. Oelrichs changed into his swimming costume and jumped overboard. He bobbed among the five-foot swells, the ocean floor one thousand feet below him. The sharks approached curiously. Oelrichs thrashed in the water, making as much commotion as possible. When the sharks came near, he punched at them—and one by one, they swam away.

Today, scientists learn about sharks in many ways. They observe sharks in their natural environment. They attach tracking devices to them to discover where they travel. They study sharks' DNA in high-tech laboratories.

In Hermann Oelrichs's time, scientists mostly studied dead sharks that had washed ashore or been caught in fishing nets. So until the 1916 attacks, Oelrichs's 1891 encounter was taken as scientific proof that sharks weren't dangerous.

In 1915, nearly ten years after Oelrichs's death, the *New York Times* published an article about the unsettled $500 bet. It claimed the idea "that sharks can properly be called dangerous, in this part of the world, is apparently untrue."

The next year, three scientists published a report on sharks. Dr. Frederic Lucas, director of the American Museum of Natural History in New York City, wrote the section on the great white.

As a boy, Lucas had circled the globe with his sea-captain father. He never heard a single story of a shark attacking anyone. Nor had he learned of an attack in his many years of study. "There is practically *no* danger," Dr. Lucas

Frederic Lucas

stated, "of an attack from a shark about our coasts."

The article was published on April 24, 1916.

By the first of July, Charles Vansant was dead.

There would be more blood in the water in the days to come.

CHAPTER 5
The Second Attack

July 6, 1916—Spring Lake, New Jersey

The beachside town of Spring Lake is located about forty-five miles up the Shore from Beach Haven. It was a wealthy community, home of the Essex and Sussex Hotel, one of the country's grandest.

Essex and Sussex Hotel

President William Howard Taft

Talk around town that summer had turned to politics. The hotel had just hosted former president William Howard Taft for its Fourth of July celebration. A few miles up the Shore at Long Branch, President Wilson would campaign for reelection from the front porch of Shadow Lawn, the "summer White House." Wilson's staff set up offices in nearby Asbury Park.

Charles Vansant's death had not discouraged visitors from flocking to Spring Lake. Many people believed it could have been just a sensational newspaper story. Vansant, they assumed, had probably just drowned.

Twenty-eight-year-old Charles Bruder, the hotel's head bellhop (an employee who helps guests with their luggage), also didn't believe a shark had attacked Vansant.

Bruder was born in Switzerland and had worked in the Spring Lake hotels since he was a boy. He worked hard and loved his job, and he dutifully sent his tips back home to his mother. He had also lived in California and swum with sharks many times, and had never been harmed.

A former soldier in the Swiss army, Bruder was tall, blond, and muscular—and an impressive long-distance swimmer. On the afternoon of Thursday, July 6, once the hotel guests had returned from the beach to bathe and nap in their rooms, Bruder gathered some coworkers for a quick swim.

He stopped at the lifeguard station. Talk turned to sharks, but Bruder assured the lifeguards he was unafraid. When he swam past the beach's safety lines, no one stopped him.

NO BATHING
BEYOND ROPES

A crowd gathered. Long-distance swimming was a spectator sport, something exciting to watch and to write home about. Before long, Bruder was twelve hundred feet from shore.

Suddenly, Bruder was hit from behind with overwhelming force. Blood and foamy water exploded high into the air.

At first, people didn't realize what had happened. One woman called to the lifeguards that a red canoe had capsized. She thought the fountain of blood was a red boat!

At the sound of Bruder's bloodcurdling screams, the two lifeguards dropped their rescue boat into the surf and began rowing as fast as they could.

After the first strike, the shark returned to Bruder. It bit down on his left leg and pulled him under, shaking him violently. The shark released him, then clamped down on his other leg. One witness said Bruder was tossed in the air between strikes.

"A shark bit me!" Bruder cried as the lifeguards approached. He was struggling to stay afloat in a sea of his own blood. The lifeguards reached down to pull Bruder out.

They were surprised at how light the man felt.

Both of Bruder's legs had been bitten off at the knee!

A chunk of his abdomen had also been ripped out. The flesh around his wounds was torn to ribbons.

One lifeguard tried to stanch the bleeding
with his shirt while his partner rowed to shore.
Bruder lost consciousness.

Some scientists say the attack on Bruder was characteristic of a great white shark attack. Nine out of ten white shark attacks are quick, violent, and come from behind. (Bull sharks, another species known to attack humans, typically approach slowly before an attack.)

SHARK KILLS BOY ON JERSEY SHORE

500 Bathers See Charles Bruder Attacked by Man-Eater —Both Legs Taken Off

Spring Lake, July 7.—A shark bit both legs off Charles Bruder in the surf here yesterday afternoon and in its vicious strokes otherwise wounded him so that he died soon after being taken ashore. He lived long enough, however, to tell a remarkable story of his encounter.

Bruder, seventeen years old, was a bell boy in the new Essex and Sussex Hotel here. He was a very strong swimmer and always went far out beyond the life lines.

The boy was about 100 yards off shore when Captain White heard him cry for aid. He saw him go under the water twice and then come up, and those two times under the water proved to be when the shark took off the legs, one at a time.

Back on the beach, doctors had rushed to the scene.

But Charles Bruder was already dead.

CHAPTER 6
Hysteria

Within a half hour of Bruder's death, urgent calls had been made to neighboring communities warning about the man-eating shark. Thousands of bathers along thirty miles of coastline fled the water.

The next morning, the beaches were empty.

Hotel pools filled up. Towns along the New Jersey coast installed steel netting around their beaches. Waves of visitors cut their vacations short.

Boats full of men armed with guns and harpoons patrolled the waters. They baited hooks with hunks of meat and tossed buckets of bloody chum overboard, hoping to catch and kill the shark.

In the newspapers, reports from the battlefields of World War I were replaced with articles about the attack. "Shark Kills Bather off New Jersey Beach!" read the front page of the *New York Times*. "Legs bitten off by maneater before guards," said the *Philadelphia Inquirer*. Political cartoons began depicting German U-boats as menacing, bloodthirsty sharks.

In the *Washington Post*, Annette Kellerman, a famous actress who had played a mermaid in a popular movie, warned Americans that ocean swimming was dangerous. She worried that the

killer shark would linger in the area, and that others might join it. "Then we will be subjected to a reign of terror," she wrote.

Shark sightings were reported all along the East Coast.

Annette Kellerman

In Bayonne, New Jersey, just across the harbor from Brooklyn, New York, a group of children spotted a shark while swimming. As the kids raced ashore, a policeman rushed toward the commotion. An eight-foot-long shark was approaching. The policeman emptied his revolver into the water, lodging a few bullets in the shark's head before it swam away.

On July 8, lifeguard Benjamin Everingham was patrolling the waters off Asbury Park in a small rowboat. It had been two days since the Spring Lake attack, and nothing had happened in New Jersey waters since. Confident he had nothing to worry about, Benjamin hadn't bothered bringing the rifle and ax he was supposed to carry on his rounds.

Suddenly, Benjamin spotted something cutting through the waves: the dark gray fin of an eight-foot shark. And it was barreling right toward him!

The lifeguard knew he couldn't row to shore faster than the shark could reach him. He leaped up, oar in hand. Just as the shark bore down on the rowboat, Benjamin struck it hard. The shark turned sideways, and Benjamin whacked it again. The shark darted away.

Benjamin rowed furiously toward shore, warning everyone about the shark. Chaos ensued as over a hundred bathers ran screaming from the water.

That day in New York City, a press conference was held at the American Museum of Natural History. Fears were growing that one shark was responsible for both fatal attacks, and that it was making its way toward the city's beaches. The museum's scientists hoped to ease people's minds.

American Museum of Natural History

Dr. John T. Nichols had examined Charles Bruder's mangled body. In his expert opinion, it was not a shark that had killed Bruder, but an orca—a killer whale. When questioned by the press, Dr. Frederic Lucas said: "No shark could skin a human leg like a carrot, for the jaws are not powerful enough." Two deadly attacks less than a week apart were highly unusual, the scientists said. The chances of a third attack were practically nonexistent.

Four days later, the scientists would be proven wrong.

Dead wrong.

Killer Whale vs. Killer Shark

Orcas are the oceans' other apex predator. They are also the only animal known to feed on great white sharks! How do they do it? It's believed that the orca first stuns the shark with a blow, then grabs the shark in its mouth. It turns the fish belly-side up and holds it in place, preventing water from pumping over the shark's gills. This drowns the shark.

Orca attacks great white shark

Then the orca can tear open the shark's belly to get at its nutrient-rich liver, the only part of the shark orcas tend to eat.

Sometimes, orcas hunt in groups, increasing their chances for success. Two male orcas have been hunting white sharks off South Africa's Gansbaai coast since 2015. Anytime the two orcas, named Port and Starboard, make a kill, the area's white sharks dive deep, flee the area, and sometimes don't return for months. The Gansbaai coast was once well known for its white-shark population. Tourists visited to observe the shark population from inside diving cages. But until orcas Port and Starboard move on, the sharks are reluctant to return.

CHAPTER 7
Matawan Creek Massacre

On Wednesday morning, July 12, retired sea captain Thomas Cottrell set off on his daily walk. The captain lived in Keyport, a town on Raritan Bay, which separates New Jersey from New York City's borough of Staten Island. It is about forty-nine miles along the coastline from Spring Lake.

Cottrell moved briskly for a man of fifty-eight. His walk took him over a trolley bridge spanning the mouth of Matawan Creek, which emptied into the bay at low tide. With a full moon just two days away, the tide was unusually high. Salt water flowed inland, up the creek, toward the town of Matawan.

Something caught the captain's eye in the muddy waters beneath the bridge: an eight-foot-long dark-gray shark. And it was heading inland, away from the bay!

Why would a shark swim upriver into a freshwater creek?

Perhaps it had been following the curving New Jersey coast and mistook the two-hundred-foot-wide mouth of the creek as another bend in the shoreline. Soon, Matawan Creek would narrow to twenty feet. At high tide, the creek was at most eight feet deep; by low tide, it would be only one.

The captain could scarcely believe his eyes. But he remembered hearing about Renny Cartan, the boy who said he'd been clipped by a shark the day before.

Cottrell had to get word to town, *fast!*

He ran to the bridge keeper's office and called John Mulsoff's barbershop in Matawan. Mulsoff was also the town's only policeman. He and the men in the shop laughed at the captain's story. "You have a better chance seeing an elephant cooling off down there than a shark," one joked.

Frustrated, Cottrell rushed to his motorboat, the *Skud*. He sped up the creek, warning everyone he saw and hoping he'd beat the shark to Matawan. Red-faced and gasping for breath, Cottrell reached town and sounded the alarm up and down Main Street, before returning to the *Skud* to patrol the creek.

A couple hours later, eleven-year-old Lester Stilwell and his friends were swimming in Matawan Creek. It was ninety-six degrees, and the boys couldn't resist the cool water.

Lester Stilwell

Freshwater Sharks?

Of the more than five hundred species of sharks, only a handful can survive in fresh water. The most common—and dangerous—is the bull shark. Sharks require salt in their bodies to keep them afloat. In fresh water, they lose salt. But bull sharks' kidneys recycle salt within their bodies, enabling them to thrive in fresh water. Bull sharks have been caught

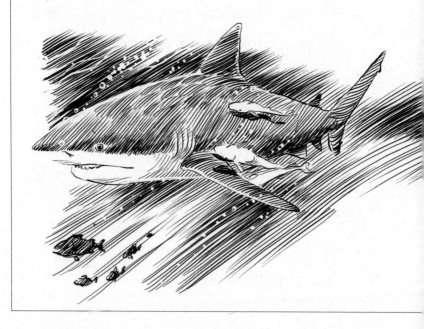

as far as 1,750 miles up the Mississippi River—and 2,500 miles up the Amazon!

Some believe the Matawan Creek shark might have been a bull shark. Only great white and tiger sharks have attacked more humans than the bull. But others believe it could have been a great white, or another species, following the salt water of the ocean's high tide. While a saltwater shark could not have survived long in the creek, it could have survived long enough to attack and retreat.

Bull shark

Suddenly, Lester's friend Albert "Ally" O'Hara felt a sandpaper-like object scrape his leg.

Then another boy, Charlie Van Brunt, saw "the biggest, blackest fish he had ever seen" cruising toward Lester.

Just as Lester was telling his buddies to watch him float, the shark struck.

Great white sharks can leap up to ten feet in the air when attacking prey.

A man sits inside the jaws of a megalodon, a prehistoric shark
(American Museum of Natural History publication, 1901).

A group of men at the beach on the New Jersey shore, 1916

Beachgoers in New Jersey swim using safety ropes in the early 1900s

Postcard from the Elephant Hotel in Atlantic City, built in 1881

Advertisement for Atlantic City, 1925

Postcard of beachgoers enjoying the water in Beach Haven, New Jersey

Women working as lifeguards in the early 1900s

People at the beach in Spring Lake, New Jersey, 1920s

One of Woodrow Wilson's presidential reelection campaign vans, 1916

Newspaper articles about the shark attacks of 1916

Actress and swimmer Annette Kellerman (1886–1975) as a mermaid

An orca, or killer whale, catches a sea lion close to shore.

The bull shark, which can survive in fresh water, is a potential culprit in the 1916 shark attacks.

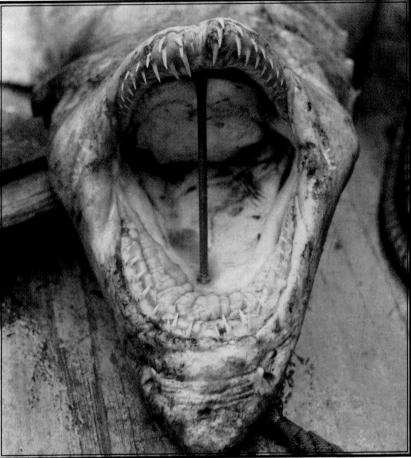

A shark killed in New York during the 1916 "war on sharks"

Peter Benchley, author of *Jaws*

View of Raritan Bay between New Jersey and New York's
Staten Island, 1900s

Steven Spielberg (second from the left) and crew filming the movie *Jaws*

Reinhard Dirscherl/ullstein bild/Getty Images

Divers photograph a great white shark from the safety of a cage.

A shark warning sign on a Massachusetts beach, 2021

Australian protesters speak out against the use of shark nets.

In a flash, the great fish twisted, exposing its white belly to the horrified boys as it shook Lester as a cat shakes a mouse. It dove, swatting its tail so hard against Ally that it slammed him against the pilings beneath the pier. Moments later, Lester surfaced, shrieking and waving his arms, before being pulled back under.

The boys ran to Main Street, naked and muddy, screaming: "A shark got Lester!"

Constable Mulsoff rounded up a search party. He figured that Lester—who was epileptic—had probably had a seizure and drowned.

The boys hurried to Stanley Fisher's shop. Twenty-four-year-old Stanley was a tailor, and a friend to all the kids in town. He was Matawan's best athlete and could always be counted on when the boys needed a ninth player for baseball. The boys knew Stanley would agree to help them.

Stanley Fisher

Stanley closed shop and changed into his bathing costume. He grabbed two men—George "Red" Burlew and Arthur Smith—and headed for the creek.

Men in rowboats trolled the creek bed,

hoping to locate Lester's body. Chicken wire was strung across the creek, so Lester wouldn't be pulled out by the tide.

Stanley, Red, and Arthur began diving. The Stilwell family watched from shore.

Near the dock, Arthur felt something rough scrape his belly. Blood seeped through his shirt.

Deep in the middle of the creek, through the murky water, Stanley saw Lester's body under what he believed was a log. Stanley took a deep breath at the surface and dived down again. He grabbed hold of Lester and swam back up.

By now, two to three hundred people had gathered along the banks of the creek. When Stanley emerged holding Lester's pale and lifeless body, the crowd gasped. Parents covered their children's eyes.

Stanley was in waist-high water when the shark bit his right thigh. He dropped Lester's body as he tried to keep his balance, kicking and punching ferociously.

Men in rowboats rushed over. Stanley broke free multiple times, only to be yanked underwater. The boaters swatted at the shark with their oars, hoping to distract it long enough for Stanley to escape.

At last, Stanley surfaced. The shark recaptured Lester's body and dragged it into the depths. As Stanley was pulled to shore, the chicken wire spanning the creek fell.

Blood spurted from an eighteen-inch wound on Stanley's leg. He had lost ten pounds of flesh— and buckets of blood. Some onlookers fainted.

A doctor on the scene didn't believe Stanley would survive the bumpy car ride to the hospital. Stanley was whisked to the train station on a makeshift stretcher. The next train wouldn't arrive for more than two hours; the closest hospital was another two hours away.

Miraculously, Stanley survived the trip—only to die after five minutes on the operating table.

Thirty minutes and three-quarters of a mile from the attacks, another group of boys was playing in the creek: twelve-year-old Joseph Dunn, his older brother Michael, and their friend

Jerry. A man on shore called out, warning them about the shark.

The boys swam to the dock. Jerry and Michael scrambled up the ladder. Joseph was only ten feet from safety when the

Joseph Dunn

shark attacked. "I felt a tug," Joseph later said, "like a big pair of scissors pulling at my leg." The shark thrashed in the shallows, struggling to drag Joseph into deeper water. Michael jumped in to save his brother.

By now, a small fleet of boats had joined Captain Cottrell. Jacob Lefferts, a thirty-four-year-old Matawan lawyer, reached the boys first. He leaped into the water, fully clothed, to help Michael rescue Joseph. Somehow, the two managed to pull Joseph from the shark's jaws.

As they hauled Joseph up the ladder, the shark returned for a final, vicious bite, stripping the flesh from the boy's leg. After a heroic battle, Joseph was freed once more, and the shark—fighting against shallow waters and a falling tide—wriggled its way back to the creek's center and headed for the bay.

Joseph was loaded into Cottrell's boat and brought to a car, which sped him to the hospital.

He survived, and the doctors were able to save his leg as well.

When word of Joseph's attack and Stanley's tragic death at the hospital reached Matawan, the town erupted. Hundreds of angry men and factory workers marched to the creek carrying hammers, axes, guns, and dynamite. They shot at

the water and set off explosives; dead fish floated to the surface. They trolled for Lester's body. By nightfall, fifteen nets were strung across the creek to capture the boy's corpse before it washed out to sea.

The people of Matawan were under attack. It was time to go to war.

CHAPTER 8
War on Sharks

News of the Matawan Creek attacks spread fast. Sightings were reported all along the Eastern Seaboard. While surely some were real, many were likely imagined. It seemed as if shark panic gripped the entire nation.

Two large sharks were allegedly seen near Tarrytown, New York, more than thirty miles up the Hudson River. While swimming off Brooklyn's Coney Island, a famous actress named Gertrude Hoffman said a shark nearly attacked her, but she beat the water and scared it off. And Florida fishermen claimed they had never seen as many sharks before in their lifetimes as they had that summer.

Gertrude Hoffman

New Jersey's governor urged towns to install netting around their beaches. Desperate not to lose any more business, many towns did. "We Are Fencing Our Beach with Wire," one advertisement read. "Come Down and Laugh at the Sharks!"

Many people, however, preferred just to kill the sharks.

"A new sport, and public service . . . has spung up," the *New York Times* reported. "The hunting of sharks." The desire for revenge spread like fever. Dozens of sharks were hooked, dragged ashore, and cut open in front of curious onlookers. One fishing party caught a bull shark more than nine feet long, ten miles from the mouth of Matawan Creek. Its stomach contained twelve shark pups but no human remains.

Two days after the attacks, Lester's partially eaten body was found floating in the creek. He and Stanley Fisher were buried the next day.

In the following days, the town of Matawan filled with shark hunters and curious lookie-loos. At one point, nearly a hundred cars lined the creek. An almost party-like atmosphere ensued.

"Fashionably dressed women and girls from Jersey coast resorts tripped down to the water's edge to watch the shark hunters at work," reported one Philadelphia newspaper.

In Washington, DC, the congressman representing Atlantic City proposed a bill to provide $5,000 (more than $140,000 today) for "the extermination of man-eating sharks infesting" the Jersey Shore. A representative for the White House told an Asbury Park newspaper that President Wilson would do all he could to "rid the Jersey coast of the shark menace."

On July 14, the Wilson administration declared a war on sharks. The US Coast Guard would do whatever it took to make the New

GOVERNMENT TO AID
FIGHT TO STAMP OUT
THE SHARK HORROR

Jersey Shore safe. Hundreds of sharks were slaughtered. None contained human remains. And soon, this so-called "war" was called off.

By now, Dr. John T. Nichols had visited Matawan and concluded the attacks had indeed been the work of a shark. A thirty-foot-long orca, he said, could not have navigated a creek so narrow. Nichols believed a single shark

John T. Nichols

was responsible for all five attacks. His boss, Dr. Lucas, agreed. "Science Admits Its Error," read the *New York Times* headline.

But where was the shark?

CHAPTER 9
Caught!

Friday, July 14—Raritan Bay

Michael Schleisser

It was a cloudy, calm morning. Forty-year-old Michael Schleisser and his friend John were fishing in Schleisser's eight-foot wooden motorboat. They were four miles from the mouth of Matawan Creek. The friends dropped a net over the back of the boat to trawl for fish. After slowly motoring along for about an hour, the boat stopped so suddenly and with such force, the men flew forward and the boat's engine cut out.

They peered into the water. "My God, we've got a shark!" Schleisser screamed.

The shark began pulling the boat backward—then down. Water poured into the boat. John scrambled up front to weigh the boat down while Schleisser tried to cut the shark loose from the net. It turned and attacked the boat, snapping its jaws and trying to jump aboard.

Schleisser knew a thing or two about dangerous animals. He was a big-game hunter and an animal trainer for the Barnum & Bailey Circus. He even kept a black bear, a wolf, and alligators in his New York City home!

Schleisser grabbed a broken-off oar he'd found on the dock earlier. He struck the shark hard—first on the nose, then the gills. The shark charged, its mouth agape, scraping Schleisser's wrist with its skin. He continued beating the shark until finally, it died, sinking back into the net.

For a few moments, the stunned men sat in silence. Then they flagged down a boat to tow them ashore. On the dock, Schleisser cut the shark open. Along with fifteen pounds of what appeared to be human flesh, medical professionals on the scene found something interesting in the shark's stomach: a shinbone and a rib.

Schleisser was also a taxidermist—someone who dissects, preserves, and stuffs animals for display. Back home in New York, he measured the shark—7.5 feet long, 350 pounds—and got to work preparing it. He mailed the recovered bones to Dr. Frederic Lucas, who confirmed they were human.

A few days later, the stuffed shark was displayed in the window of the *Bronx Home News* office. Tens of thousands of people came to see the "Jersey Man-Eater." Schleisser stood out front with the half-broken oar, telling the crowd the story of his battle with the monster.

Dr. Lucas and Dr. Nichols were among the visitors. Nichols identified the fish as a juvenile great white shark.

CHAPTER 10
Understanding Sharks

MAN EATING FEMALE SHARK CAUGHT OFF NEW JERSEY COAST

HEAD OF MAN-EATING SHARK

After Michael Schleisser's encounter, the shark attacks stopped. Had he indeed slayed the man-eater? And had one bloodthirsty shark been the culprit in all the attacks that summer? No one knows for sure. We don't know what happened to Schleisser's shark or the contents of its stomach.

And yet, another question remains: Why?

Why would a shark, or sharks, begin attacking humans, seemingly out of the blue?

Some early theories were outlandish. One belief was that, due to ships full of sailors being sunk by German U-boats, sharks had developed a taste for human flesh. Also, that sea warfare during World War I had driven the sharks across the Atlantic, from European to American waters.

German U-boat

The "rogue shark" theory suggests that a single sick or injured shark, unable to capture its normal prey, had turned to hunting something easier: humans. This idea was supported by the story of the Tsavo lions. Over nine months in 1898, two male lions—both without manes, one with a diseased tooth—killed some thirty-five railway workers in Kenya.

Tsavo lions

Some say the unseasonably hot summer of 1916 could have drawn more sharks to the area. It had certainly attracted record numbers of human visitors to the beach, increasing the odds of encounters with sharks. That summer, scientists also observed more sandbar sharks in the region

Sandbar shark

than usual. Juvenile sandbar sharks are a favorite food of bull sharks.

One thing is certain: The attacks of 1916 changed Americans' view of sharks forever.

In the summers that followed, there were no more attacks. Memories faded, but fear no doubt lurked in the back of many people's minds.

Our fascination with sharks has only grown over time. In 1964, a fisherman harpooned a great white shark estimated at 4,500 pounds off Long Island, New York. An article about the man caught the eye of writer Peter Benchley. It would inspire

his novel *Jaws* and the 1975 blockbuster movie that followed.

Jaws is the story of a small beach town being terrorized by a rogue white shark. Town officials and business owners fear if the shark isn't killed, the summer tourist season will be lost, along with their seasonal income. A local fisherman, accompanied by the chief of police and a shark expert, is hired to kill the shark.

Sound familiar?

Jaws rekindled people's fear of sharks. In the following decades, shark populations dropped. Conservation efforts to save the sharks kicked into gear. The health of the oceans depends on the health of its apex predators. Today, great whites— and their favorite prey, seals and sea lions—are protected by law. As the animals' numbers rise, though, encounters with humans also increase.

Cape Cod, Massachusetts, has become the summer gathering spot for large numbers of white sharks, and a deadly attack occurred there in 2018. In 2020, about two hundred miles north of Cape Cod, a woman at Bailey Island, Maine, was killed, the state's first-ever fatal attack. Six nonfatal attacks occurred on Long Island in the summer of 2022, prompting beach closures.

Today, sharks and the risks of ocean swimming are better understood than they were in 1916. Beachgoers and lifeguards use drones, helicopters, and mobile apps to spot sharks. Some beaches in Australia and South Africa still use shark nets, though many people are calling for their removal.

(Their effectiveness is questionable, and many sharks that get caught in the nets die.)

Still, humans pose a much greater threat to sharks than sharks do to humans. Worldwide, people kill one hundred *million* sharks annually, many just for their fins. (Shark fin soup is a delicacy in some Asian countries.) Overfishing has led to oceanic whitetip shark populations plummeting by as much as 95 percent in some areas.

Scientists learn more about sharks every day. This knowledge—where they mate, give birth, feed—can help determine areas to protect from fishing. Great white sharks, whose DNA helps protect them against illnesses, may even hold the key to curing cancer and other age-related diseases.

If the events of July 1916 taught us anything, it was that the ocean is not our playground. It is its own ecosystem—a world to be respected, and perhaps a little feared.

What we have learned *since* that fateful summer is that to fear something is often to misunderstand it. And the more we understand about sharks, the better we can coexist peacefully with them.

Timeline of the Shark Attacks of 1916

1916

April 24 — Dr. Frederic Lucas states: "There is practically *no* danger of an attack from a shark about our coasts"

July 1 — Charles Vansant, twenty-three, attacked and killed by shark close to shore at Beach Haven, New Jersey

July 6 — Charles Bruder, twenty-eight, attacked and killed by shark 1,200 feet offshore Spring Lake, New Jersey

July 8 — Scientists downplay the danger of a third shark attack and suggest an orca may be responsible for the killings

July 11 — Renny Cartan Jr., fourteen, clipped by shark while swimming with friends in Matawan Creek, New Jersey

July 12 — A shark attacks Lester Stilwell (eleven), Stanley Fisher (twenty-four), and Joseph Dunn (twelve) in Matawan Creek; only Dunn survives

July 14 — Dr. John Nichols visits Matawan and concludes that a shark is responsible for the attacks

— The US government declares a "war on sharks"

— Michael Schleisser captures and kills a shark four miles from the mouth of Matawan Creek in Raritan Bay; later discovers human remains in its stomach

July 19–21 — Tens of thousands visit the *Bronx Home News* office to see the "Jersey Man-Eater"

Timeline of the World

1916

April 20 — Chicago Cubs play their first game at Weeghman Park (later renamed Wrigley Field)

May 31–June 1 — British and German navies face off in the North Sea at the Battle of Jutland, the largest sea battle of World War I

June 21 — US troops pursuing Mexican revolutionary Pancho Villa attacked by Mexican government troops at Carrizal

July 1 — Coca-Cola begins selling current Coke formula

— In France, French and British troops launch the Battle of the Somme against German forces

July 4 — Four immigrants allegedly hold the first known hot-dog-eating contest at original Nathan's Famous location on Coney Island

July 9 — German U-boat *Deutschland*, the first cargo submarine to cross the Atlantic Ocean, arrives in Baltimore, Maryland, after a 3,800-mile voyage

July 15 — Pacific Aero Products (later, the Boeing Company), an airplane manufacturer, founded in Seattle

July 20 — Lake View Store, first modern indoor shopping mall in the United States, opens in Duluth, Minnesota

1917

April 4 — US declares war on Germany, enters World War I

Bibliography

*Books for young readers

Capuzzo, Michael. *Close to Shore: The Terrifying Shark Attacks of 1916*. New York: Broadway Books, 2001.

Casey, Susan. *The Devil's Teeth: A True Story of Obsession and Survival Among America's Great White Sharks*. New York: Henry Holt, 2005.

Fernicola, Richard G., MD. *Twelve Days of Terror: A Definitive Investigation of the 1916 New Jersey Shark Attacks*. Guilford, CT.: Lyons Press, 2001.

*Tarshis, Lauren. *I Survived: The Shark Attacks of 1916*. New York: Scholastic, 2010.

Website

International Shark Attack File: Floridamuseum.ufl.edu/shark-attacks.